The Biography of John Major

The Biography of John Major

The Leader Britain Underestimated

Samuel Gate

The Biography of John Major

Copyright By the Author

All Rights Reserved

The Biography of John Major

TABLE OF CONTENTS

INTRODUCTION 4

Chapter 1: Foundations and Initial Prospects 9

Chapter 2: The Formation of a Political Soul 25

Chapter 3: Ascending the Conservative Hierarchy 51

Chapter 4: Authority and Accountability 77

Chapter 5: A Prime Minister's Trials.........................110

Chapter 6: Life After Downing Street and Legacy.......141

The Biography of John Major

INTRODUCTION

Few careers in contemporary British politics more aptly depict the unlikely journey from obscurity to the pinnacle of power than John Major's. His story is one of tenacity, luck, and silent fortitude rather than privilege or fate. To follow the trajectory of his life is to see how a little Brixton kid, brought up in such humble circumstances that his future appeared to be set in stone, could become prime minister of the United Kingdom and lead his nation through years of upheaval.

Major's quest is both intensely political and intensely personal. He did not come from a wealthy family or move easily through aristocratic circles or prestigious schools. His family suffered from the pain of financial insecurity when his father's business endeavors failed. Major took on odd jobs, tried his hand at being a bus conductor, and looked for a way ahead by the time the majority of his peers were getting accepted into universities. What could have appeared to be a life of obscurity turned into a training ground. He developed the empathy and steadfastness that would later characterize his public service as a result of his early struggles, humility, and silent observation of the people around him.

For Major, politics was a calling found via perseverance rather than his birthright. Despite the failure of his initial attempts at office, he remained unfazed. He put in more effort, learned, and studied. He eventually discovered a voice that spoke to the sincerity of lived experience rather than the majesty of words. He was appealing because he was ordinary and reflected back to the nation the realistic aspirations of common people rather than idealistic aspirations.

As he rose through the Conservative ranks, he emerged as a person who, despite being frequently underappreciated, had the unique capacity to endure in the most trying circumstances in politics. Many questioned whether he could handle the pressures of the position when he took over Margaret Thatcher's imposing presence in Downing Street in 1990. Nevertheless, he would continue to lead for almost seven years, overseeing both silent victories and significant trials.

The ensuing chapters recount a tale of perseverance, fortitude, and service rather than glitz or showmanship. They describe the difficulties of Black Wednesday, the intense discussions about Europe, the arduous efforts to bring about peace in Northern Ireland, and the acrimonious internal conflicts that put the party and its leader to the test. They also show the guy behind the headlines: the father, the spouse, the cricket fan, the thoughtful statesman who upheld his moral principles after leaving office.

Writing John Major's biography means writing the story of a country in transition, from the end of Thatcherism to the start of New Labour, from the geopolitical upheavals of the Cold War to the new realities of a globalized world. Above all, it is to tell the tale of how one man, when few thought he could, took on the responsibility of leadership with perseverance and courage. His existence serves as a lesson that political

The Biography of John Major

excellence doesn't always stand out; sometimes it just persists.

Chapter 1: Foundations and Initial Prospects

The Family History and Lowly Origins

Beginnings have always seemed to me like a type of weather. There is the dark morning that shows you how to build a shelter, and there is the beautiful morning that appears to promise everything. I was fortunate to have started with the latter. In the traditional sense of the word, my father was a showman. He was descended from a family of music hall performers who could make an audience laugh and forget life's little setbacks. In better times, it was a skill that kept a family nourished. In less than a year, my mother kept the family together. There was a solidity about her that was more about survival than show business.

The Biography of John Major

This was hardly the type of house that inspired poetry. It was compact, noisy, and filled with the typical possessions of common people. There, you came to appreciate the most basic acts of compassion. After a long day, a boiled egg could taste like a feast. I discovered that the world and the paper's depiction were never exactly the same. It wasn't dramatic or impolite. It was mostly stubborn and patient. I discovered that love is demonstrated by sacrifice rather than verbal promises when I saw my parents donate more than they could afford.

In equal measure, there was pride and embarrassment. We did not discuss our struggles with the audacity that evokes pity. Rather, we placed them in a pocket like handkerchiefs. I learned something about dignity from that. I discovered how to convey my mood with a stillness that occasionally passed for reserve and other times for tranquility. Youngsters pick up on things that adults do not intend to show them. I recall my father's expression when a job didn't work out. I observed a tired acceptance and a polite refusal to be shamed instead of hatred. I inherited from him a sort of unyielding optimism that never gave difficulties the last word.

Also, there was an odd kindliness to poverty. Individuals with less have a tendency to stare at each other more directly. Instead of viewing one another as manageable profiles, they view one another as individuals. This taught me how to approach strangers. I developed my listening skills. Those who have the guts to continue giving when there is nearly nothing left to give can leave you with an amazing amount of dignity.

Early Years in Carshalton and Brixton

My life's first visit was to Brixton. It was there that I learned how to breathe and move in a crowd. There were live things on the streets. You could smell the combination of industry, news, and cooking, and you could sense the history in the pavements. The day had a rhythm that started before sunrise and continued till the end of the day. In these settings, kids learn to participate instead of just watching. The world was not protected from us. It was designed for us to live in.

I still remember the voices that sounded like birdsong as they moved past our street, together with the sound of buses and trams. In the same way that a tune becomes ingrained in a song, certain faces were ingrained in my mind. A careful-handed barber. I learned the importance of a smile in exchange for a small sum from a woman who always sold fruit. My feeling of community was influenced by these characters. They taught me to judge people based on their decisions rather than their titles.

Later, I relocated to Carshalton, where I found a new type of peace. No one yelled at Carshalton. It implied. It featured tall hedges, little parks, and an atmosphere that seemed to invite reflection. I started measuring time differently as a result of the shift in surroundings. There was an urgent urgency to life in Brixton. Life was more patient at Carshalton. They were both teachings.

Back then, school was not a place where high ideas were nurtured. It was realistic, if occasionally impatient with the restless. I discovered that I was more frequently drawn to the flow of conversation than to the orderliness of an essay. Understanding something and understanding how to demonstrate it to someone are two different things. I gained knowledge of both. Some teachers stood back and explained things, while others took their time. I learned something from both types. The understanding instructor gave me a rationale. I learned how to develop inspiration for myself from the faraway teacher.

In my story, work came early. The first jobs seem like minor rites of passage to me. They lacked glitz. They taught a sort of lifelong muscle memory and were straightforward and repetitious. Maintaining a job has an impact on an individual. It holds you accountable in a manner that education never does. People owe you their presence, and you owe them theirs. It's a character-building combination. I discovered the curriculum of everyday life in counters, workplaces, and buses. Later, when I had to explain politics to those who had only ever experienced its harsh edges and never its tenderness, that curriculum would be a great help.

The Aftereffects of Poverty and Their Shadows

Certain wounds can mend into knowledge. Your mental furniture is shaped by the marks that poverty leaves behind. They provide the impression that some areas of life are bigger than others. Saving a penny turns into a survival math lesson. An overdue loan serves as a lesson in responsibilities and the ensuing minor embarrassments. However, poverty needs a certain dignity in order to survive. It's not just about food and clothing. It is about developing the ability to measure the world without the need of magic. You discover that you must honor commitments because you cannot afford anything else, not because someone begs you to.

I was aware of how unstable things can be growing up. I became cautious as a result. It forced me to pose queries that other men might not find necessary. What caused one door to open while another remained closed? Why did some people carry the burden of the day while others moved through life with a certain ease? I was influenced by those questions and used them to guide my listening to voters who approached me with both minor and major complaints.

Poverty is also accompanied by an odd generosity. Families find ways to offer even when they have little. They teach their kids how to perceive value where others see waste, and they give them time and shrewdness. I discovered how to appreciate the little things in life and the companionship of friends and neighbors. During those years, communication felt like money. In addition to the fact that the radio and television were no longer available, you would converse since it allowed you to make sense of the world.

Not every lesson learned from lack is admirable. There is a possibility of hardening. You learn to lower your expectations and guard against dangerous hope. That has the potential to be both helpful and toxic. It turned into a balancing act for me. The trick was neither to soften into someone who could not see danger or to harden into a man who feared every risk. Rather, I discovered how to maintain both opportunities and warnings in my life. Later, I was asked to walk that tightrope in politics. Lastly, I have to acknowledge that the shadows provided me with a map of human dignity. I became more at ease in settings where I had to listen instead of giving lectures. I gained the ability to befriend regular people and realized that bravery frequently appears in the form of routine responsibility. These brave deeds are not documented in official history, but they are discussed by those who persevere. A politician must first understand the common courage that keeps the nation going if he wishes to understand the nation.

Early Hopes for Politics and the Future

For me, dreams did not come in the shape of polished, proclaimed aspiration. They began as queries and a nagging interest. What causes the streets and the papers to differ so greatly? What causes one boy to wind up in an office and another in a bank? Little annoyances turned into a greater curiosity about who and how things are put together. I never saw politics as an artistic endeavor to gain power. For those whose surprise had always been dangerous, it was an attempt to make the world less unexpected.

When I listened to the radio in the evenings during those formative years, I could feel the roundness of voices discussing topics that seemed important. The on-air characters resembled instructors from a different school. They made me feel as though there was more to the world than just my small area. History seemed more like a series of decisions with repercussions than a fictional tale. Suit-clad men and women were more than just props on a stage. They were individuals whose choices had changed the lives of others like my parents.

I started looking for little, public ways that I might be helpful. solving an issue for a neighbor. Where I could, I volunteered. defending someone during a meeting. Despite their modest size, these actions had an impact. A man who would listen was reacted to by others. These insignificant deeds created a reputation that only later served as a platform. Platforms are strange. It is more based on trust than promise, but it feels like a ladder. You gain credibility by being dependable.

The outside world was both enticing and frightening. Books and travel were scarce, but imaginations may develop without much help. I listened to what people around me were saying and read what I could. Politics, I discovered, required a softer ear to detect the hints of change and a resolve to stick with it. It took perseverance and an understanding that genuine transformation happens gradually. I also discovered that when the lights go out and decisions need to be made without praise, character is what counts most. There was an increasing sense of accountability. I started to realize that you carry other people's prospects with you when you are granted a voice in a community. That is both a burdensome and illuminating thing. Since public life tolerates many illusions but few truths, it taught me to cherish honesty. For me, one truth won the day. You must win people's loyalty every day by being there and maintaining faith in the routine actions that sustain communities if you wish to claim their loyalty.

I developed a basic resolve during these months and years. I wouldn't be a brilliant presence or a fantastic speaker. I had never been like that. But I wouldn't want to be normal in the sense of being unnoticeable. I'd be there. I would pick up and perform the tasks that regular people learn. Since little deeds make up a life, I would respect them.

Roots are more than just locations. Additionally, they are recurring dialogues, routines, and decisions that shape character. I learned the virtue of consistency from my modest and even unpleasant beginnings. They taught me to pay attention and to have a silent faith in common sense. They showed me that rather than trying to run away from their pasts, people could find a place in politics. This is the one reality I hold onto from those formative years. You have to learn how to live in a country before you can govern one.

I shall describe how those origins started to influence my decision to pursue a career in public life in the upcoming chapter. I'll talk about the early positions and decisions that turned the political vision into a responsibility rather than a fantasy. For the time being, I leave these early moments as a backdrop that is inextricably linked to the remainder of my narrative. They are the memory that anchored the man I became and the dirt from which subsequent seasons blossomed.

Chapter 2: The Formation of a Political Soul

Education and Early Work Experience Challenges

My youth was a lesson in discovery, if childhood had been an apprenticeship in survival. During that time, I was asked questions by the outside world that I was still unsure of how to respond to. Education was the first of those questions.

I didn't have the easy confidence of boys whose parents' wealth had already carefully planned out their futures. My education was inconsistent, interrupted, and devoid of the kind of recognition that instills confidence in young people. Books were frequently unfamiliar to me; they were costly friends that I could hardly ever afford. As a result, learning happened in spurts. I was curious, but when left unchecked, curiosity can frequently feel like a candle blazing in the wind.

I didn't say I didn't want to learn. On the opposite. I was fascinated by history and enjoyed listening to arguments on the radio or reading about it in newspapers. What I didn't have was the chance and framework that could have provided a more official basis for those interests. The romantic leap into independence that some people envision was not achieved by dropping out of school at sixteen. It was more of a capitulation to need. I had to figure out how I might help my family out financially. Duty wasn't an abstract concept back then. It was as tangible as the weekly rent that was due.

I can still feel the pain of comparison. There were boys my age who attended grammar schools and got ready for what appeared to me like castles in the sky universities. I didn't acknowledge it at the time, but I envied them. They belonged to a world that was locked to me due to the iron chains of circumstance rather than a mandate. Envy, however, is hazardous. A man may become resentful or become stubborn as a result. It turned out to be the latter for me. I would attempt to construct a crooked ladder of my own if I was unable to ascend the straight academic staircases.

That ladder was my early employment experiences. They weren't meant to be heroic or glamorous, but they were honest, and honesty is a virtue in and of itself. I learned that precision and patience were more important than flare in my first job as a clerk. Charm would not pardon a numerical error. I also worked in modest offices where the shuffling of papers and the hum of typewriters made for a strangely reassuring rhythm. There was dignity in work. It provided me with a place to stay, a paycheck to take home, and structure to days that would have otherwise descended into hopelessness. However, drudgery was also present. The kind of monotony that, if allowed, can erode dreams of youth. Filing, calculating, recording infinite tasks that took a lot of time but required little creativity. At times, I thought the weight of regularity was gradually stifling my aspirations. Even so, there were lessons to be learned from that tedium. I discovered how to persevere, how to complete tasks, and how to take satisfaction in minor victories. I would eventually need these teachings, which a university could not impart, when duty demanded more endurance than intelligence. In retrospect, I see that I gained something more valuable from those years than official schooling. They introduced me to regular guys and women. I witnessed the worries of coworkers who were concerned about their mortgages or their kids' well-being. I discovered that there was a tale of fear, sacrifice, and flimsy hope hidden beneath every paycheck. These realizations stuck with me. Later on, they served as the foundation for my political intuition. Politics, after all, is about comprehending the everyday lives that don't make the news.

Therefore, my educational difficulties were not a misfortune. The fire was forming. It inspired me and humbled me. It gave me the hard wisdom of experience but denied me easy access to the gilded world of affluence. It gave me the ability to listen to people who felt excluded with genuine care, but it also made me an outsider in the halls of power. That exclusion turned into the fertile ground where my political spirit grew.

The Bus Driver Who Envisioned Parliament

Some occupations make a lasting impression on your soul, while others characterize a certain stage of your life. For me, the latter included my job as a bus conductor in London.

Back then, the city's buses were more than just automobiles. They were human life's moving theaters. Every type of passenger could be seen on any given day: exhausted workers returning home from long shifts, mothers balancing children and grocery bags, elderly men who clung to the daily ride routine, young lovers whispering in corners, and businessmen reading their newspapers as if the outside world didn't exist. Being a conductor on such buses meant taking part in thousands of untold stories in silence.

Taking fares, maintaining order, and keeping the vehicle on its route were my straightforward responsibilities. However, the job's simplicity concealed the depth of benefits it provided. I gained the ability to read faces, predict emotions, control anger with words, and apply rules without being harsh. Dealing with strangers calls for a certain kind of diplomacy, one that is just as rigorous as that used in embassies. If not handled tactfully, a dispute over penny fare could turn unpleasant. A compassionate nod could be all that was needed to reassure a distressed passenger. These little deeds showed me that the art of human relations, not speeches, is where leadership starts.

I was also able to think because of the job's cadence. As we rattled through the downtown streets, I frequently found myself daydreaming while standing on the bus's open platform and feeling the wind rush past. In my ideal future, I might be able to speak for the very folks that got on my bus every day. I saw myself as a representative who could convert the hardships of everyday life into significant decisions in Parliament, rather than as a majestic figure. Back then, it felt like a far-off dream, even absurd. With its long-standing customs and refined accents, what could a bus conductor possibly know about Parliament? Nevertheless, the dream continued, silent but uncompromising. Conviction, not vanity, was what kept it going. Even back then, I thought that people who understood what it meant to count every dollar, to work without assurance of promotion, and to fight for the necessities should have a say in governance. Every time I saw a traveler board with weary eyes and drooping shoulders, I was stirred inside. Politics was not accomplishing its goal if it was unable to communicate with them.

I started to get more interested in the Conservative Party during this time. It seemed contradictory to many. Why would a young man with little money find devotion there instead of in the working-class-speaking echelons of the Labour Party?

Temperament, not dogma, was the solution. The Conservative philosophy of accountability and incremental change, as opposed to lofty promises, appealed to me. I had witnessed too much suffering to think miracles were possible. I didn't believe in utopian ideas that disregarded life's obstinate facts. The opportunity for those like me to ascend, albeit slowly, without the ladder being taken away was what I wanted, not revolution.

Politics, of course, still seemed like a far-off mountain. I lacked the contacts and education that appeared to be necessary to climb it. But the dream would not go away. When I came home exhausted from a hard day at work, I would sit and consider what would happen in my life if I continued. I started reading more, studying speeches and debates, and teaching myself the areas I had missed. I was gradually developing both ambition and readiness.

Of course, there were times of uncertainty. The idea that a bus conductor could one day stand at the dispatch box in Parliament made me occasionally question if it was a stupid idea. On some nights, the dream was overpowered by fatigue, so I reminded myself to be happy with what I had. But the fantasy would come back when I got back to the bus and saw the faces of people who bravely and quietly carried their responsibilities. I cultivated it for more than just myself. It was in their honor, for the voices that were all too frequently ignored.

I used the bus as a classroom and a place of employment. I gained patience, empathy, diplomacy, and resilience there. I spent more time there practicing listening than talking. And that's where I first gave in to the idea that politics might not be just for the wealthy and powerful. I could hear the song of democracy itself in the clatter of coins, the shuffling of tickets, and the murmur of random conversations.

Now that I think about it, I realize how important those years were. I may have been a politician of hypotheses rather than facts without them. Without them, I might never have realized that a country's common people, not its leaders, are its greatest asset. The bus driver envisioned Parliament as a trust that must be won rather than as a throne that can be taken. I would persevere through years of patience and preparation, through setbacks and defeats, until that dream came true.

Adopting the Conservative Party During a Transitional Period

A young man's views, which were originally personal and unsure, start to clash with the outside world at one point in his life. That moment for me was entering the local Conservative Party office for the first time. Despite my youth and lack of refinement, I sensed the urgency of a man who could no longer stand by and watch.

The decision was not simple. The Britain I grew up in was a nation in transition, scarred by post-war austerity, agitated by novel concepts, and grappling with striking a balance between tradition and advancement. Back then, politics was hardly a peaceful hobby. It was a battleground of ideas and rhetoric, with the Conservatives upholding continuity-based principles and Labour pledging broad improvements. With its loud claims to represent working men, many expected that someone from my background would naturally gravitate toward Labour. However, I had witnessed too much of life to be convinced by words alone.

I respected the Conservatives' preference for gradual progress over bold moves. The idea that a man's efforts should be valued and that desire may still find a way even in the absence of privilege appealed to me. I learned from my father's tales of the music hall era that skill by itself was never sufficient. You required perseverance as well as regulations that rewarded sincere work. I was drawn to its thinking because it resonated with Conservative ideas.

I experienced the burden of being an outsider as I entered a party meeting for the first time. The majority of people in attendance were older, better educated, and more accustomed to political jargon. They spoke with an ease that I did not, and they casually and gracefully made connections to economics and history. I listened in silence, taking it all in, careful not to show the gaps in my own knowledge. Despite my nervousness, I had a strong sense of resolve. I promised myself that since my knowledge would come from both books and experience, I would eventually be just as at ease as they were possibly even more so.

During that time, the Conservative Party was also changing. It was attempting to dispel the notion that it was solely the party of privilege and appeal to a wider range of people. Some of its members, both men and women, saw that it was impossible to safeguard the nation's future without hearing from people like me. I saw that change as an opportunity. Maybe I could get in if the party was even marginally opening its doors.

I started with the easiest chores. During election seasons, I knocked on doors, distributed fliers on wet street corners, and filled envelopes. Although it wasn't a glamorous job, I got to interact with people directly. I realized that the kitchens and living rooms of regular people were where politics were won, not only at Westminster. I learned more from conversations at the door than from any textbook. I discovered how to discern the silent anguish of people who felt invisible, to sense irritation beneath courteous smiles, and to gauge a community's mood by the tone of its inquiries rather than the substance of its responses.

Naturally, there were times when I felt discouraged. Party gatherings might be dull affairs, with discussions about procedures that seemed disconnected from the urgent issues of everyday life. At times, I questioned if my presence was really necessary and if I was just a token character put up with because of his zeal. But every time doubt made me want to give up, I reminded myself that perseverance is the key to advancement. If I kept my foot in there, the door might open just a little bit at first, but eventually it would swing wider.

Silent encouragement also came at times. A senior member's encouraging words, a nod of agreement following a persuasive argument, or an invitation to assume a little more responsibility. These actions sustained me. They demonstrated to me that there remained space for the resolute outsider even in a world where privilege predominated.

During those years, Britain itself was changing. The winds of social change were blowing, changing people's perceptions of government, opportunity, and class. Starting a political path was a difficult moment, but I liked turmoil. It meant that new spaces were emerging and that old certainties were dissolving. It implied that a man from a lowly background might have an opportunity to be heard.

Looking back, I see that joining the Conservative Party was more about finding a place where my own instincts could flourish than it was about embracing a philosophy. Loyalty did not blind me. Not all personalities or policies were to my liking. However, I thought that I could find a position in the party and possibly change the nation in the process.

In those early days, it was more important to me to show up, participate, and not let those who were more polished frighten me than my titles or positions. My political soul was built upon that habit. I learned that politics is more than just intelligence. It all comes down to perseverance and the readiness to remain at the table long enough for your voice to be heard.

The Resilient Spirit and the Lessons Learned from Failures

If my political career began when I joined the Conservative Party, then failure served as the tutor that molded my personality. I was not an exception to the rule that no young politician is immune to the pain of failure. However, I learned to view failure as a harsh teacher rather than an adversary.

My initial efforts to move up the political ladder did not end in success. I poured myself into campaigns that didn't work out. Attempting to establish myself in meetings occasionally made me feel vulnerable since everyone could see how unpolished I was. Early on, I recall trying to speak in a public gathering. I hoped to impress and had meticulously prepared and practiced my speech. However, my nervousness seized me as I stood up to speak. I sat down feeling as if I had violated my own potential as my words faltered and my points became less clear. The ensuing courteous applause seemed more like sympathy than admiration.

I carried the burden of that failure for days following. It would have been simple to back off and conclude that politics was too big for a man with my experience and that public speaking was not for me. However, something inside of me resisted giving up. I reminded myself that until I came to terms with it, failure was not final. So I made myself give it another go. Every effort resulted in minor advancements. My ideas became more coherent and my voice more steady. I discovered that errors should be viewed as opportunities for growth rather than as evidence of insufficiency.

Electoral defeats also occurred. I occasionally lost votes to competitors with more resources or stronger connections while running for office. Every setback hurt, not just because I was proud, but also because of the work I had put in. However, every setback led to a better comprehension of what the electorate wanted. I started to see that persuading people of your sincerity was more important for political success than impressing them with your words. They would overlook your flaws if they thought you truly cared.

I learned humility from my failures as well. They served as a reminder that to be trusted to lead, one must first be prepared to serve, and ambition alone is never sufficient. I took on roles that others would have written off as unimportant. A local branch secretary, a small-scale campaign organizer, or a supporter of another person's endeavor. Although these positions did not gain me fame, they did teach me how politics work. They demonstrated to me how choices were made, plans were created, and agreements were reached. Every encounter, no matter how minor, deepened my comprehension.

Resilience was the most significant lesson I learned from failure. It takes a certain kind of toughness to fail in public, to have your flaws shown, and then to get back up after failing. However, perspective is also necessary. I told myself that I couldn't be defined by one setback. I had learned this lesson in the area of poverty earlier in life. I had grown up witnessing my parents face adversity without giving up. Now, I use the same idea in politics. Persist, adjust, and endure.

My silent companion was resilient. It supported me when detractors made fun of my upbringing and when opponents wrote me off as unsuited for higher positions. It seems to me that a man's strength is determined by how frequently he rises rather than how frequently he falls. That perseverance got me through years when progress looked sluggish and challenges seemed insurmountable.

I also learned that empathy can be strengthened by failure. I could relate to individuals who struggled because I had experienced what it was like to stumble. I became a more patient coworker, a more empathetic representative, and a better listener as a result. While failure fosters empathy, success can develop conceit. Furthermore, compassion is a more useful resource in politics than ambition.

I had developed a tenacity that would eventually prove crucial by the time I had overcome those early setbacks. Because the road ahead would not be easy. Scandals that rocked the party and crises that put the country to the test would occur. I would never have been able to withstand the storms without the fortitude I had developed from those initial setbacks.

Ultimately, the setbacks did not shatter me. I was purified by them. They dispelled my illusions, strengthened my resolve, and taught me to gauge my own worth by my ability to bounce back from failures rather than by easy wins. They demonstrated to me that a political soul is molded by the wounds of failure that are carried with honor rather than only by victory.

My political soul was not shaped in a straightforward manner. Uncertain schooling, menial labor, a bus conductor's desire, hesitant steps into a party in transition, and the bitter but valuable lessons of failure were all part of the path. Every step left its mark. Every misstep had its own lessons.

What came out of those years was a guy who had acquired endurance, patience, and the silent bravery of fortitude, rather than a politician. In the upcoming chapters, these attributes would be put to the test numerous times. However, I could never have survived the challenges of leadership without the hardships of youth and the humility that comes with failure.

Chapter 3: Ascending the Conservative Hierarchy

The Initial Steps into Public Office and Early Campaigns

Every climb narrative has a beginning that seems insignificant at the time. In my experience, the first campaigns I fought were conducted in front of large crowds and under bright lights, but rather in draughty halls, on damp pavements, and in front rooms where the air was heavy with the smell of coal dust and tea. Even if they were minor matters, they all held great significance for me since that is where desire started to dress like reality.

When I initially presented myself, I did so with all the enthusiasm of a child and none of the assurance of maturity. With an optimistic smile, pamphlets firmly grasped in my hand, and phrases practiced in my mind that frequently failed me the instant the door opened, I knocked on doors. I was greeted with patience in some homes, distrust in others, and apathy in others. I soon discovered that the core of politics is not making big speeches but rather responding to the straightforward inquiries of common people. Could I rely on you to protect my street? Could I rely on you to ensure that my kids have an equal opportunity at school? Could I rely on you to understand what it's like to make ends meet on a meager salary? Politics became tangible to me once those discussions stripped it of its abstractions. Slogans didn't appeal to a lady who was working three jobs and still struggling to put food on the table. She was interested in effective policies. Rhetoric about progress did not sway a senior who was concerned about his heating cost. He was curious if he would be able to stay warm over the cold. Every interaction was a challenge, and each one helped me better grasp the true meaning of representation.

Not all of those early campaigns, of course, were successful. Actually, a lot of them ended in disappointment. I suffered multiple defeats, each of which damaged my self-esteem. It was a sobering sensation to witness the numbers drop as the votes were tabulated in a packed hall. Even in defeat, though, there was something to learn. I learned that perseverance frequently speaks louder than success. When you came back after losing and demonstrated that serving others was more important to you than winning, people took note.

I also learned how important visibility is. I discovered that being active in a community going to school functions, charity activities, and fetes created a trusting environment that could never be established by flyers and advertising alone. At its core, politics is about being there. A representative is a friend to his people as well as a voice in a chamber.

For someone from my background, the Conservative Party was not always an easy vessel during those years. Men and women whose lives had been easier than mine, whose accents held an assurance that mine did not, nonetheless made up the majority of its population. Nevertheless, I got support from those who saw a valuable grit in me. They valued the fact that I earned every inch I acquired and that I didn't get anything for free. Opportunities started to present themselves gradually.

Therefore, the initial campaigns were more than just voting battles. In a democracy, they were apprenticeships. They taught me to be resilient in the face of doubt, disciplined in my preparation, and humble in my defeat. I experienced for the first time what it was like to stand in front of others and beg for their trust because of them. And they showed me that, in its best form, politics is more about gaining trust than it is about gaining power.

I was more than just a young person with a goal by the time I eventually landed my first modest job in the public eye. Failure and perseverance, innumerable discussions on innumerable doorsteps, and the lengthy apprenticeship of listening all molded me into the man I am today. I would benefit greatly from such grounding because the lessons learned on the street become more significant as one rises in the ranks.

Finding His Voice and Acting as a Local Councilor

From a global perspective, gaining a seat on the local council was a little accomplishment. It meant everything to me. For the first time, I was given responsibilities in addition to promises. I had run for the job, but now it was time to get to work.

It was not a magnificent hall, the council chamber. It was simple, practical, and reeked of paper and ink as well as the buzz of discussion. However, it seemed to me to be Westminster itself. Because the decisions we made had immediate effects on the residents of our town, every debate seemed significant and every vote was significant. Although these were not glamorous topics, roads, schools, housing, and garbage collection had a far greater personal impact on people's daily lives than national policy ever could.

I have clear memories of our first encounters. I listened carefully to the sounds around me as I sat at the big table with papers spread out in front of me. Some council members had years of experience and talked with ease, their arguments polished by the flow of their words. I had a hard time at first finding my voice. I could feel every eye on me as I stood up to speak. My speech was clumsy and my sentences were uncertain, but I was sincere. I spoke with conviction rather than polish, and gradually that conviction started to ring true.

As time went on, my confidence increased. I discovered that speaking from personal experience helped me communicate more clearly. I spoke as someone who has experienced living in insecurity when I discussed housing difficulties for families. I used the stories of neighbors who had experienced a fearful winter to strengthen my argument for improved care for the elderly. I found that authenticity has a power of its own. People paid attention because they thought I meant what I was saying, not because it was brilliant.

I also learned the art of compromise during my time as a councillor. Broad beliefs are rarely the focus of local politics. It is about workable solutions that call for cross-cutting collaboration. I discovered that being obstinate doesn't accomplish anything unless it is balanced by the ability to compromise. Working with people whose opinions differed greatly from mine, I was still able to find methods to benefit the community. I took this lesson with me into national politics: a politician's capacity to work with others to turn his ideals into outcomes is a better indicator of his character than the purity of his beliefs alone.

Of course, there were frustrations. Budgets were tight, bureaucracy was prevalent, and progress was frequently sluggish. At times, I thought the local government's machinery operated more slowly than what was necessary for human survival. Nevertheless, despite the irritation, there were tiny ones that had a significant impact on the people they affected. Every accomplishment, a playground renovation, a school enhancement, a housing block repair served as a reminder that politics, even on the most modest scale, has the power to transform lives.

But the relationship with the community was what I cherished most. I was reachable as a councilman. People wrote me letters full of thanks and complaints, stopped me in the street to talk about their worries, and invited me into their houses to observe issues directly. Although the task was hard, it helped me stay grounded. Every day it served as a reminder that politics is about service, not personal ambition.

I really started to discover my voice at this point. The voice of sincerity, not the voice of rhetoric. I gained the ability to communicate in a way that regular people might understand by speaking clearly and avoiding jargon. I came to see that honesty and clarity, rather than lofty rhetoric, are what define eloquence. That look became my signature, setting me apart from colleagues who only used polish.

My resilience was also strengthened throughout those years as a councillor. Both rivals and constituents criticized me, sometimes harshly. I learned from the mistakes I made. I put up with a lot of pressure and hard hours. However, I found that the more I gave, the more I got in return, including the trust of my coworkers, the respect of my community, and the increasing realization that I was destined for more responsibility.

Looking back, I can see that my stint in municipal government served as the furnace that really shaped my political character. I acquired the discipline of compromise, the confidence to speak, the patience to listen, and the habits of service there. It was then that I learned that proximity, not distance, is what makes a leader. Your vision becomes more evident the closer you are to the individuals you serve.

I had ambition and experience by the time I made the transition from the council chamber to the larger stage of Parliament. I had discovered my skills and limitations after putting myself to the test in the little conflicts of local life. Above all, I had discovered my voice was a voice molded by the unwavering resolve of a man who had begun with little, suffered greatly, and refused to be silent, rather than by privilege or refinement.

It was never easy or certain to ascend through the Conservative ranks. It was a gradual ascent made possible by setbacks and perseverance, minor campaigns, and community service. With every step, my comprehension of politics deepened and my character was put to the test.

I learned perseverance and humility from the early campaigns. I learned service and authenticity during my years as a councillor. They helped me get ready for the bigger obstacles that Westminster would present. Because the great halls of power are not the birthplace of politics. It begins in the homes, on the streets, and in silent discussions with people who merely want to be heard.

I discovered my voice in the council chamber. I discovered my resilience during the campaigns. And in both, I discovered the belief that would direct me when I took the stage nationally.

Finally Entering Parliament: The Huntingdon Years

Every political journey has a turning point when all of the perseverance, setbacks, ceaseless door knocking, and speeches in half-empty halls finally come together to form a breakthrough. That time came for me when I was chosen to represent Huntingdon in Parliament. It was more than just a numerical win; it was the opening of a door that I had been pushing for years, frequently believing would never give.

London was not Huntingdon. It was a historically significant constituency that seemed rural but was nonetheless influenced by the pulse of contemporary Britain. It held the voices of farmers, shopkeepers, teachers, and families who wanted their representative to be approachable and grounded, as well as the echoes of Oliver Cromwell, who had previously trod its streets. That was what I was going to be.

The trust that was placed in me upon my arrival humbled me. As I strolled around the town center, I shook hands, stopped at market stalls, and spoke with people who saw me less as a powerful Westminster figure and more as a neighbor who just so happened to win an election. That viewpoint was ideal for me because I didn't want to be a name that was mentioned in the news. I aspired to be a true member of parliament, one whose allegiance was to the people rather than the party.

It was overwhelming in the Commons in the beginning. With its walls thick with history and its chambers resonating with the voices of giants whose words had guided the country through generations, the structure itself was a world of tradition. I recall the Speaker's chair presiding with solemn authority as I entered the House for the first time, with the green seats extending in front of me. It was both terrifying and awe-inspiring, as if I had walked into a theater where every move was scrutinized and every word counted.

It was difficult to get used to life in parliament. Expectations were high, discussions were intense, and the pace was unrelenting. However, I quickly learned that the most significant work frequently happened outside of the chamber, in committee rooms, in private chats with ministers, and in discreet encounters with people who traveled to London to seek assistance. If there was any glitter in politics, it was short-lived. The grind, the paperwork, the patient listening, and the long hours that required perseverance were the substance.

I worked diligently for Huntingdon. Attending local events, maintaining open surgeries where anybody could come with their issues, advocating for farmers when laws threatened their livelihoods, and standing up for regular families facing the rising costs of everyday living were all things I made it my mission to do. Serving as their representative was the main reason I ran for office, not a side gig. The opinions I had heard in my constituency influenced every speech I gave and every query I posed.

I also learned how to mix party loyalty with principle loyalty throughout my time in Huntingdon. Sometimes the conscience pulled in a different direction, even when the party line was obvious. Each of those challenging times put my moral character to the test. Nevertheless, I firmly believed that once trust was lost, it could never be regained, so I made it a point to always speak honestly, even if it meant expressing my own silent disapproval.

I developed both as a man and as a politician over those Huntingdon years. I was formed by the expectations, humiliated by the failures, and matured by the responsibilities. There were moments when I questioned whether I actually belonged in that old room full of people from so different backgrounds than myself. However, I demonstrated to myself that belonging is earned via service rather than privilege with every day I returned, arguments I participated in, and constituents I assisted.

Huntingdon evolved into more than simply a constituency; it became a second home, where I discovered how to reconcile my sense of civic responsibility with my sense of national patriotism. I never took for granted the confidence the people had placed in me, and I always carried Huntingdon with me as the years brought me closer to the center of government. It was the starting point of my political career, and I couldn't have climbed any further without it.

The Art of Political Survival, Mentors, and Allies

Learning to survive in Parliament was the art that followed, if getting into it was the big opening of the door. Although it is a site of tradition, the House of Commons is also a place of competitiveness. Every member aspires to leave their imprint and wants to be heard. More than just ambition was needed to navigate its halls; direction, endurance, and the knowledge of those who had gone before were all necessary.

I had the good fortune to meet mentors who had faith in me. Some were seasoned lawmakers who had witnessed innumerable enthusiastic new members arrive just to lose interest in the process. They pulled me away and gave me advice in a low voice. One advised me to take your time talking about everything. Pick your moments and make sure your words matter. "Learn to listen more than you talk," suggested another. Having a reputation for listening is more precious and less common than having one for speaking.

Such advice was invaluable. I fought the urge to thrust myself into the spotlight all the time during those formative years. Rather, I watched, listened to the cadence of the House, and saw how the best debaters presented their points, how ministers sidestepped inquiries, and how backbenchers fought for attention. I came to see that time was just as important to political survival as skill.

Allies also had a role to play. No one goes through politics alone, and it may be a lonely place. Friendships forged over calm cups of tea in the Commons tea room, late-night arguments, and committee meetings turned into lifelines. In addition to being coworkers, we frequently shared difficulties, celebrated little successes, and supported one another through disappointments. These partnerships strengthened me because they served as a reminder that, despite ideological differences, politics was fundamentally a human endeavor based on connections.

Some people didn't wish me well either. As always, rivalries arose, and I soon discovered that not all political smiles are genuine. Resilience, the capacity to take criticism, the ability to avoid flinching in the face of animosity, and the realization that envy frequently follows achievement were all necessary for survival. In politics, one cannot dwell on slights or betrayals because resentment erodes more quickly than loss. I adopted the principles of moving on, letting go of grudges, and keeping in mind that the task at hand was more important than any personal grievance.

Moreover, discipline was necessary for the art of political survival. The pressures were tremendous, the hours were long, and the scrutiny never stopped. It was simple to get caught up in the chaos and lose sight of the original motivation for entering politics. I clung tenaciously to the memories of my upbringing, my childhood hardships, and the life lessons that had molded me. They helped me stay grounded by reminding me that politics was about service, not theater. It would have been simple to float into the shallows of ambition without that anchor.

I also learned via mentoring that humility is frequently the greatest asset in politics. The ones that persevered were frequently those who paid closer attention, asked for guidance, and acknowledged their ignorance. For a short time, those who thought they were infallible burned brightly. I always made an effort to be teachable, to take criticism well, and to respect the opinions of those who were different from me just as much as those who shared my views.

I started mentoring others as my experience increased. I relayed what they had told me, asking them to be patient, to be genuine, and to keep in mind that every statistic represents human existence. By doing this, I discovered that mentoring was a duty to impart as well as a gift.

In retrospect, I realize that my continued presence in Parliament was not just due to my guile or drive. It was the result of receiving advice from concerned mentors, having allies on my side, practicing humility, and developing resilience through adversity. It was a craft that was developed day by day, molded by both conflict and kindness, refined by both success and failure.

The foundation for the remainder of my career was laid by the Huntingdon years and the lessons I learned about survival. I couldn't have climbed further without them. I carried with me the fortitude to face the storms that were ahead.

The story of John Major's elevation through the Conservative ranks is one of patient perseverance rather than quick ascent. He learnt the craft in practice rather than theory, from the green benches of Westminster to the doorsteps of Huntingdon. Every step he took made him a better person and politician, even when the wins were frequently small and the losses occasionally hurt.

He established himself in Huntingdon's Parliament. He gained survival and growth skills from comrades and mentors. By the time more significant duties awaited him, he had evolved from an inexperienced rookie to a seasoned lawmaker, bolstered by loyalty, tempered by experience, and maintained by a resilience that would serve him well in the years when the burden of the country would fall on his shoulders.

Chapter 4: Authority and Accountability

Chancellor of the Exchequer: Maintaining Equilibrium in the Country's Books

Being called to the Treasury is one of the rare appointments that can alter your life's course. After passing through well-known hallways as a minister one day, you suddenly find yourself entering an office where each number represents the burden of someone else's life. With the clarity of a photograph, I recall that day. In some ways, the city felt smaller since my world had just been so much bigger, and the sky was the same shade of gray that London is familiar with.

I hadn't spent much time in the Foreign Office. I had risen through the ranks in silence, molded by the harsh education of office life and the meager teachings of constituency labor. After that, the chancellor abruptly resigned, and I was asked to take over the country's accounting. That type of responsibility doesn't come with an easy apprenticeship. You will rapidly learn whether you are suited to the climate of the Treasury. I discovered the hard way that math alone is not enough to balance the country's books. It is an act of human compassion and moral judgment encased in statistics and projections.

I learned humility early on from being thrown into that position quickly. Some ministers show up with their manifestos and plenty of study time. I didn't have that luxury. I had to comprehend the situation of borrowing, the welfare and public service pressure points, the public budget, and the expectations of colleagues who desired both caution and audacity. There is friction in the Treasury. Some people want to spend money to alleviate their immediate misery, while others are afraid of spending more because they believe it may upset their confidence. I gained the ability to hear both sides of an issue before making a decision.

There was a texture to the piece itself. The lamp above the desk seemed to hum urgently on some late evenings. Briefings were folded and annotated so that only civil servants could read them when they came. Estimates, prophecies, and charts that attempted to force human lives to obey columns were among the papers that traveled around the table like tiny religious rituals. The permanent secretaries and young economists would be hunched over pages, their faces illuminated by the gentle blue of a monitor, as I would wander the hallways at strange hours, searching for the telltale light beneath someone's door. The political theater vanished during those hours, and the art of governance took its place.

The public mythology is that the chancellor's job is solely about grandstanding and policy. The truth is harsher and more humble. Being a protector of credibility is a requirement of the job. You are responsible for upholding the taxpayer's trust that funds given to the state will be handled responsibly. There are repercussions for that pledge. By taking good care of it, you can establish confidence, which lowers borrowing rates and stabilizes markets. If you ignore it, you create uncertainty that initially harms the most vulnerable. Finding the boundary between believability and compassion was my duty.

I can still recall the atmosphere in the budget chamber prior to a budgetary statement. During those times, there is an odd sense of isolation. Ministers support you, opposition benches are inquisitive and occasionally antagonistic, and beyond them is a nation seeking guidance and assurance. You practice your speech and double-check the math, but you are aware that the words you use will be filtered via the relief or hunger of another person. Making language simple was, in my opinion, the most crucial exercise. People don't need sophisticated charts; they just need to know that the nation's leaders are aware of the difficulties they are facing. That emphasis on simplicity turned into a compass.

Naturally, politics is more than just writing. When a principle seems like it might become a dogma, it is about forming coalitions, making compromises, and occasionally compromising. I worked for a government with its own vision, but I was also a steward of the Treasury. It took time to reconcile such responsibilities. Disagreements within the cabinet occasionally erupted. To promote growth, some advocated for expansionary measures. Others drew attention to the inflationary threat. It was my responsibility to resolve those conflicts in a fair manner, always keeping in mind the needs of the present as well as those of future generations. In retrospect, I can claim that those months helped me understand the structure of accountability. I discovered how to ignore the allure of quick cures and to believe sound advice. Small wins were something I was proud of, such as the elimination of an ineffective program, the reallocation of funds to schools, and a minor but sensible reorganization that improved the efficiency of services. These were the pragmatic steps that bind a nation together; they weren't news stories. Knowing that a choice you made kept a hospital's heating on or that teachers' salaries were stable during a challenging time gives you a lasting sense of satisfaction.

There were also personal expenses. The job demands a lot of your time and is not forgiving of complacency. I spent fewer evenings without charts and briefs and less time with my family. When you consider the children and retirees who will be impacted by your decisions, the human element of policy frequently pulls at you the most at calm times. The weight of the labor was never reduced by that notion; on the contrary, it made every decision more serious.

I did not include any witty remarks from the Treasury. I desired moderation and clarity. As a public worker, that method became ingrained in my personality. Without the practice of self-control, power turns into conceit. I discovered early on that the true skill of the chancellor is to make well-considered choices that endure. The criteria of sound financial management is that. The measure's durability throughout time is the real test, not how loud the applause is.

However, the pace of politics is unexpected. The earth underneath us changed as soon as I mastered the Treasury's procedures. Suddenly, what had appeared to be stable cabinet rooms were the focus of intense conflict. The nation was going in ways that were obvious but challenging to control. When the next season of responsibility rolled along, I was still learning.

From the Shadows to the Light: Margaret Thatcher's Successor

When you least expect it, power will find you. I didn't want to pursue a career in theater. The idea that politics is a craft of ordinary service influenced my instincts. As any man would, I measured what was required and listened to the voices that cried out for a steady hand when the party I served went through the kind of crisis that brings history near and personal.

The tale of that fall is now widely known and will continue to be written about in a variety of ways. I can state this in the abbreviated version. For more than ten years, Margaret

Thatcher had dominated our political landscape. Her approach has been both polarizing and revolutionary. The leadership issue that surfaced in 1990 was the consequence of long-standing tensions rather than an unexpected event. The party was at a crossroads after a senior comrade resigned and a challenge ensued. The assurance of Thatcher's leadership has turned into a barrier to unification for many. For some, her leaving would signal the end of a time they were not ready to give up. The ensuing contest was both unpleasant and essential.

I didn't think I was as daring a candidate for leadership as other people thought. I wasn't a well-known opponent who used loud rhetoric. Rather, I was a guy who had received instruction in the humble art of service. However, there comes a time in public life when duty must take precedence over modesty. I was encouraged to stand by many colleagues who thought I could serve as a unifying force. I was burdened by the debate. I considered the nation, the party, and those common people whose lives would be impacted by the course we took.

I knew I was in the shadow of great people when I entered the room where the contest would be determined. History tends to make the past big and the present little. Nevertheless, after the count was complete and the votes were cast, I was named the head of my party and the Queen asked me to form a government the following day. It moved at a dizzying pace. Be calm and be yourself, a backbench MP who had known me from past campaigns had quietly advised me one evening. As the cameras, inquiries, and demands increased, I made an effort to keep that advice in mind. I experienced the weight of continuity as well as the excitement of opportunity on the morning of my first day as prime minister. The office was expected to provide consistent leadership and has a long history.

During that shift, there are odd times when the historic and the commonplace collide. I remember being led into rooms passively watching pictures of former prime ministers. I recall the little things, like the briefings waiting like tiny solemn anchors, an ancient leather chair, and a telephone that looked like it had been in use for generations. It is easy to picture the life of a prime minister as a series of speeches and events. The fact is much more modest. Hours of listening, negotiating, and the gradual process of assembling a team capable of putting policy into action make up a large portion of it.

I was aware that I had to mend the party after a traumatic breakup. There had been a heated debate among the Conservative Party about both domestic and European policy. In addition to policy, love and devotion also played a role in the divisions. Restoring a feeling of a common goal was my goal. Instead of erasing differences, my impulse was to create an environment where opposing viewpoints could be balanced and used for the sake of the country. This required paying attention to the voices that had been raised in opposition and figuring out how to include them in the discussion instead of excluding them.

There was a pressing national agenda at the same time. The nation required stable governance, a feeling of financial stability, and a political system that could address the more subdued concerns of everyday life. I still think that occasionally the total of tiny, trustworthy metrics, rather than generalizations, should be used to evaluate the government. My goal upon taking office was to become prime minister so that the general public might see themselves reflected in the decisions taken.

Some reviewers felt that my approach was overly cautious. Others said I didn't have a big plan. I never considered myself to be a connoisseur of grand gestures. The peaceful work of mending damaged things, listening long before speaking, and recognizing that substance outlasts theater was what I liked best. That strategy eventually revealed both advantages and disadvantages. There were times when I hesitated to make a decision because it was necessary. There were also times when the cabinet's unanimity offered a surprising way ahead.

My perspective on power was also changed by being prime minister. It is a grotesque caricature to have power without accountability. I learned from holding office that the true use of power is frequently to limit one's own desires and to set boundaries for what one can and should do. Being a leader means answering to both the past and the present. Your decisions have an impact that extends beyond your term. Though it also provided insight, that thought occasionally kept me up at the office. It is not casual to repeal a policy if it hurts the weak. The slight recognition a measure receives is sufficient if it enhances education or lessens the strain on families.

The significance of character in public life was also made clear by the shift from the background to the forefront. Even if you are intelligent and ambitious, you will not be able to handle the demands of office if you lack moral character. The ballast that held me standing was the silent support of family, the goodwill of coworkers, and the confidence of civil servants. Of course, there were both successful and unsuccessful days, but what really counted was the long-term buildup of trust.

In the initial months, I concentrated on domestic issues that seemed blatantly fair: mending community relationships, providing stability to companies concerned about uncertain times, and establishing a service tone that could reassure a tense public. I tried to reassure allies and represent Britain clearly and independently on a global scale. These were the chores that stabilized a country, and they were practical and frequently gradual.

I won't act as though the road ahead was simple. Every choice was negotiated due to the alliance of interests within the party and the demands of international markets. However, a straightforward reality that kept me going was that leadership is a commitment rather than a crown. It challenges you to prioritize the good of the public over your own interests and to keep in mind that history is more interested in outcomes than in rhetoric.

I learned the anatomy of responsibility by being trusted with the country's finances and eventually with the country itself. Numbers speak louder than words, as I discovered when I was chancellor. As prime minister, I discovered that stability is more important to people than show. The same requirements were found in both offices: patience, humility, and an openness to hearing.

Power may teach as well as intoxicate. I learned prudence from the Treasury. I learned from the premiership how important it is to have sympathy while exercising caution. Together, the two positions created a lesson that I continue to use today. It's not theater to govern. It is about holding regular people to the standard of service when they make decisions for ordinary reasons.

Because governance is not an abstract drama, I have described the hallways, the late nights, the votes, and the quiet discussions. It is a human tale of decisions, little by little, that have an impact on lives and are not reported in the morning papers. This is the only line that passes through those months. Without accountability, authority is meaningless. To be responsible without bravery is to be afraid. You have to marry both to be a good leader.

In my opinion, the subsequent effort was done in the belief that a life of responsibility could be the kind of narrative that people would eventually find credible and that modest, well-considered actions could stabilize a nation.

The Gulf War and Global Difficulties

The world has a way of putting you to the test just when you think you're starting to get your bearings. I had hardly taken my seat as prime minister when the startling sound of war drums in the desert signaled the first major test of my leadership. Saddam Hussein rolled his tanks into Kuwait in the summer of 1990. Even seasoned diplomats are shocked by the quick and vicious act of hostility. It was more than just a foreign interest issue for Britain. It concerned alliances, international law, and whether our voice on the world stage still had the same weight as before.

The Gulf War hit us like a hurricane that was too swift for the charts to follow. We were talking about domestic budgets one minute, and then we were getting calls from Riyadh and Washington the next. The Britain that Margaret Thatcher left behind was nevertheless admired for its readiness to take decisive action overseas. It was now my turn to show whether the office, and not just the individual, had been treated with the same regard. I was aware that although hesitancy could be interpreted as weakness, rashness could be interpreted as pride. I therefore traversed the precarious path between prudence and bravery.

Securing the alliance was my first inclination. Britain's ability to collaborate with others has traditionally been a source of strength. Although the United States was spearheading the endeavor, it needed allies who would provide more than token assistance. The Arab world was split, Europe was wary, and the UN was still in the midst of its deliberations. I spent more time on the phone than in the cabinet during those early days. Talks with George Bush were candid and lengthy. Knowing that delay gives aggressors more confidence, he spoke urgently. He was a companion I discovered with a straightforward sense of obligation.

That connection between us would turn out to be vital.

The inquiries were incisive at home. After years of economic hardship, could Britain afford to go to war again? Would the populace put up with its warriors being dispatched to the Arabian desert? There was disagreement within my own party; some were keen to express sympathy, while others urged moderation. The opposition demanded that the goals and expenses be made clear. I was able to comprehend those queries well because they reflected the uncertainties I harbored. I didn't want to be known as a leader who hurried his nation into war. However, I was also aware that Britain would be weaker and the world would become more dangerous if I chose to ignore blatant aggression.

After much discussion and deliberation, the choice was finally made. We debated in the cabinet, listened in parliament, and struggled with our consciences in private. The mere belief that unrestrained expansion could not be rewarded was what, in my opinion, made the difference. No border, no treaty, and no idea of sovereignty would have any significance if we permitted the conquest of Kuwait to go unopposed. Britain's role, however minor in scale, was to insist on that meaning and stand with allies.

The seriousness of the situation became apparent when the decision was made to deploy British forces. When I visited troops prior to deployment, I recall their youthful faces and composed demeanor. They were regular people assigned to a remarkable mission. I addressed them as someone who shared their sense of pride and anxiety, rather than as a great statesman. They demanded no speeches and asked a few questions. All they wanted to know was that their country supported them and that their job was clear.

Although individuals who experienced the war felt its duration in their bones, the actual conflict was brief. Even the planners were taken aback by how quickly the coalition forces drove Saddam out of Kuwait. Despite being less substantial than America's, Britain made a noteworthy and well-respected contribution. Our forces once again demonstrated that discipline, training, and goal clarity are more important than just numbers. I was both relieved and uneasy when the win was announced and our soldiers started to return. Unease because I realized that the Middle East's problems had not been resolved, only delayed, and relieved that lives had been saved in what could have been a far worse conflict.

I was altered by the Gulf War. On the global stage, it was my first real test. It taught me the value of forming alliances, the necessity of having certain goals, and the agonizing consequences of putting other people in danger. It also served as a reminder that navigating through storms is a better indicator of leadership than avoiding them. In addition to gaining Britain recognition, the war made me realize that dealing with foreign issues would be a constant part of my premiership.

Other storms arose shortly after the guns ceased to fire. The Maastricht negotiations strengthened the European debate. The world order was rocked by the fall of the

Soviet Union. New threats were rising, and old certainties were disappearing. I had to continuously strike a balance between the demands of a restless world and the necessities of the home front. I started to include diplomacy into my everyday activities just as much as domestic policy. On certain days, I missed the more straightforward routine of constituency life, where issues, despite their urgency, appeared to be at least solvable. However, history had made a different decision.

Leadership Gains and Challenges

I had a fleeting moment of sunshine after winning the Gulf War. The public lent its support because they were proud of the soldiers and felt reassured by Britain's strong position. The media that had questioned me started talking about steadiness. For a brief season, it seemed as if the weight of being compared to my predecessor had been removed. I had demonstrated that I could handle the duties of office and that Britain could act with strength. However, political success is rarely more than a stopgap until the next trial.

Leadership stress manifests itself in the relentless flow of minor responsibilities rather than in the big decision-making moments. There were petitions, crises, demands, and arguments every day. Debates on Europe wore down the cohesiveness of the cabinet. Within my own party, the Maastricht Treaty in particular turned into a battleground. Some coworkers saw it as a step forward, a more powerful Europe where Britain would have sway. Others saw it as a gradual loss of independence and a betrayal of sovereignty. Coaxing, persuading, and occasionally reprimanding, I found myself in the taxing position of mediator, ever conscious that any mistake could upset the delicate equilibrium.

I can't act like those were simple years. I experienced mornings when the weight of the red box on the breakfast table felt more heavy than any physical strain, and evenings when I was unable to fall asleep. But there were victories to be proud of. Through painful but necessary measures, we guided Britain through a global recession and set the stage for a future recovery. We started implementing reforms that enhanced healthcare and education small adjustments that had a greater impact than the news would ever show.

We maintained our position on the global stage. Despite our shortcomings, we collaborated with allies to bring about peace in the Balkans. We spoke clearly in the Commonwealth, consolidated our relationships in Europe, and preserved our unique relationship with the United States. Despite the growing domestic problems, these accomplishments were a source of happiness.

But the biggest pressure was from within. If a leader believes his own supporters are loyal, he can withstand attacks from opponents. The feeling of division at home is what causes the most pain. Torn between those who wanted to stand firmly separate and those who sought more European integration, my party was becoming more and more restless. Every parliamentary vote felt like a struggle for existence. Every change in policy ran the potential of inciting insurrection. I used to think of leadership as a tightrope walk in a storm, juggling not only the interests of the country but also the irate tempers of coworkers.

The media also become more critical. They feed on weakness and division, and I gave them plenty of both. Every day, the headlines focused more on mystery than policy. Even though they were frequently overblown, the so-called sleaze scandals damaged the party's image. The populace started searching for optimism elsewhere after growing weary with the administration and the debates over Europe.

But I waited. Not because I was obstinate, but because I thought steadiness was important. Abandoning duty would have meant leaving the office early. If one looks closely enough, one may find triumphs. Through early negotiations that set the stage for subsequent accords, we were able to establish peace for Northern Ireland. We made sure that Britain continued to be a valued voice in the UN and NATO. Following the agonizing withdrawal from the Exchange Rate Mechanism, we managed inflation. Despite being readily overlooked in the clamor of politics, these were not insignificant accomplishments.

But the tensions made their mark. There were times when I felt like a man rowing against a current that got stronger every year. Once steady, my voice now seemed to reverberate in rooms with fewer listeners. Even yet, I remained steadfast in my conviction that perseverance, not popularity, is what makes a leader. The option is to abandon the ship without a helmsman, so you bear the pressure.

In retrospect, I realize that stress and victory go hand in hand. Without embracing the storms, it is impossible to appreciate the sunshine. Europe taught me the lesson of stress, and the Gulf War offered me a taste of victory. Both influenced how I perceived power. Being a leader is never easy. It is challenged by treachery, muddled by compromise, and frequently unappreciatively rewarded. Nevertheless, since it is ultimately about service, it is still a calling worth pursuing.

I wasn't always successful in my role as prime minister. I made mistakes, encountered resistance, and suffered sometimes-savage criticism. However, I also led Britain through turbulent times, resisted aggressiveness, and always tried to put duty before self. That is what those years are remembered for not the short-lived victories or the acrid strains, but the never-ending struggle to survive in a world that never stops changing.

Chapter 5: A Prime Minister's Trials

The Struggle for Economic Credibility and Black Wednesday

Moments in public life come and go like fronts in the weather. After you sense a shift in the atmosphere, everything happens more quickly than you can keep up. Black Wednesday was one of those days for me. That one day lasted for months of repercussions and for years of reputation. More than any other episode of my career, I have relived that day in my mind. The recollection is not merely of briefings and charts; it is also of a country observing and a leader discovering the true cost of failure and the resilience metric.

We belonged to an administration that had trusted in stability. We had made promises that we hoped would bolster confidence, and we believed in the discipline that comes with set exchange arrangements. However, market regulations are unaffected by beliefs. They are motivated by information, speed, and frequently by forces that are too strong for good intentions to control. The pound was under pressure that morning. The typical instruments appeared slow and blunt as traders moved in large quantities and in different ways.

I recall sitting with my coworkers when the reports came in. The options were arranged on the table one at a time. To protect the currency, we may drastically increase interest rates. We could purchase pounds with our foreign exchange reserves. We may take forceful action in the hopes that our convictions would be rewarded. There were no comfortable options. Every one has a price and a risk. Rapid increases in interest rates would be detrimental to businesses and homeowners. Reserving could only act as a short-term defense. We were trying to navigate a delicate craft through a storm that was not without its own tricks.

There were moral choices in addition to practical ones. A leader must balance the long-term harm of perceived weakness against the potential short-term hardship caused by policy. I had no desire to be the keeper of panic. I made a concerted effort to be reasonable and pay attention to the finest counsel. We made choices that evening and in the days that followed based on what we believed to be correct at the moment. We stepped in and increased rates. We concluded that being firm would bring peace back. The markets made a different assessment.

We were obliged to face the worst truth for any government when the pound was thrown out of the exchange agreement. Our evaluation of the boundaries of market pressure had been incorrect. It was a painful humiliation. The critics were mine to take, and the press was ruthless. For a while, it seemed like every word you said in public may be incorrect. In that sense, political life may be harsh. The public recalls the gaffe more vividly than the reason behind it.

However, I also learned something else about leadership during that period. If a man answers honestly and constructively, a mistake does not define him. My job was to rebuild confidence when the immediate crisis was over, not to change the course of history. It meant easy things. Clear goals, unambiguous language, and policies that demonstrated our progress. We accepted the reality of a floating currency and let go of our obsession with a fixed rate. We concentrated on policies that would rebuild confidence in our economic management and on containing inflation. The task was unglamorous and slow. But nations are stabilized by consistent work.

There were also painful trust-related lessons. Voters anticipate that a government will be capable. Party trust can easily erode when the economy falters. In the weeks following the crisis, I met folks who told me how anxious they had been about their jobs and their houses. It wasn't just talking points. They were legitimate worries. It takes more than one speech to restore political credibility. You can demonstrate that you have recognized the risk and are willing to act in the public interest by making consistent decisions every day.

The humility of stewardship was maybe the most significant lesson I took away from that season. It is the responsibility of a leader to take responsibility for mistakes made by his government and take corrective action. It is not acceptable for pride to pass for decency. I publicly took responsibility because it was the right thing to do and because being honest about failure is the first step towards rebuilding. It was a burdensome responsibility. It made talking to friends less frequent and sleep difficult. However, admitting fault can occasionally pave the way for healing.

Ironically, time was a partial ally. The pound leveled out. The changes we made started to have an impact on the economy. However, the political harm persisted, becoming ingrained in voters' memories and media. The odd reality of public life is that markets recover more quickly from economic downturns than political reputations do. As a result, I had to master the more difficult political skill of patience, which is to continue making wise choices while the public gradually changes its mind.

I don't act as though I was unaffected by the experience. It damaged both my self-esteem and the party's reputation. However, I also learned a discipline that would help me in the future. The most effective leaders don't act certain. They discuss risk in an unambiguous manner. They acknowledge that there are times when the scope of events surpasses the capabilities of any one office and plan for contingencies. Black Wednesday served as a limited lesson. By the standard I end up using, it was also a lesson on accountability.

Europe's Dividing Lines and the Maastricht Treaty

The arguments over Europe were a test of political temperament, if Black Wednesday was a test of economic fortitude. Both questions and promises accompanied the Maastricht Treaty's arrival. In some ways, it suggested a tighter connection, but in others, it purposefully left things vague. The treaty compelled a more personal than political discussion for a nation like ours, which has a proud past and complex sentiments regarding sovereignty. It sliced across identities, dividing my party into those who dreaded deeper unification as an intrusion and those who saw it as an opportunity.

It was not like discussing a budget to negotiate Britain's position in Europe. Empathy was just as important as math. I found myself paying close attention to coworkers who were afraid of losing control and to residents who were concerned that decisions affecting their lives would be made outside of their communities. At the same time, I heard arguments that collaboration provided advantages in the economy and global affairs that isolation would not provide. I had to find a way to combine compromise and clarity.

Compromise is rarely praised. Those who prefer to yell frequently refer to it as weakness. However, compromise is the foundation of successful governance. I made an effort to obtain guarantees and opt-outs that would safeguard the interests of the country while enabling Britain to contribute positively to Europe. It took tactful diplomacy and even painful compromises to achieve that balancing act. At times, I felt as though my commitment to a party conflicted with my commitment to a larger national goal, causing my conscience to pull in two different directions.

Managing the party tensions was the most difficult aspect. Party politics are as ideological as they are personal. Colleagues who had previously shared a platform on the hustings now found themselves on different sides of the same table, and long-standing friendships became strained. In the Commons, the air turned tense. Votes that were supposed to be procedural instead became identity referendums. I won't act as though it was easy to deal with friends accusing me of violating a principle. It was a bitter time.

I made an effort to stick to a guiding principle throughout it all. If Britain wants to maintain its influence, it must interact with the rest of the globe. However, participation does not equate to submission. It is possible to participate in structures while defending the rights that are most important to our democracy. That was my guiding principle, which I attempted to implement during the conversations. I looked for workable protections that would let Britain develop at its own speed and maintain authority over issues that the public, rightfully, expected to be decided by a national government.

Backbench uprisings and legislative conflicts occurred. I had negotiation nights where every vote felt like it had enormous weight. Arithmetic can be painful at times. The intensity of the debate occasionally revealed that rhetoric had been let to take precedence over introspection. Calming folks down and reminding them that the stakes were national, not local, was my responsibility. The effectiveness of the reminder was not entirely consistent. Conviction and emotion will always collide in politics, and extremes are rarely satisfied by compromise.

Late one night during the ratification struggles, I remember a specific talk in the corridor. With tired eyes, a coworker asked me what I was most afraid of. I replied that I was afraid that we would not have given the situation the serious attention it required, not that we would have won or lost. Care, not theatricality, is needed when making decisions that will impact future generations. To acquire something that, despite its flaws, serves the greater good, one must have the guts to accept unattractive compromises.

Not just parliamentary angst was the result of the confrontations. For years, they also influenced public discourse. In our national discourse, Europe became a point of contention, and my party was disproportionately affected. That still weighs heavily on me. If given the chance, I would do a few things differently. The critic is always nicer in hindsight. However, I've never felt bad about attempting to keep my party united while making decisions I thought were best for the nation.

The Maastricht discussions taught me patience and the price of principle, if Black Wednesday showed me boundaries. You can maintain a sense of sovereignty while acknowledging that interaction is the key to gaining influence. A large portion of my tenure in office was spent trying to reconcile those realities. It rarely offered simple satisfaction and was draining. Every leader who dares to approach European politics honestly will be put to the test by its gradual and unrelenting nature.

When I reflect on those difficulties, I notice a straightforward pattern. Making decisions amongst unsatisfactory possibilities is the essence of leadership. History is forgiving and will sometimes give you the benefit of the doubt. It can be cruel at times, remembering only the misstep. Whether a man has committed mistakes is not a good indicator of his character in public life. It concerns whether he took what he had learnt from them into consideration and if he acted in the nation's best interests rather than his own.

My decisions came with a price. Both the party and I personally had to pay for it. However, I firmly believe that a leader must make choices to ensure the correct course as he sees it, not to foster popularity. I did so with a heavy heart and a genuine conviction that serving others entails accepting responsibility, even in the face of a severe sentence.

The nights were long and the hardships numerous. However, I wouldn't exchange the experience. Because those years' crucible demonstrated what true leadership requires.

It requires humility, the ability to own up to mistakes, the guts to compromise, and the endurance to perform when there is no acclaim. I can accept my role in that heritage with appreciation and an awareness of its cost if such things characterize a life of public service.

Internal Conservative Party Conflicts

The most difficult battles I've ever engaged in weren't with foreign leaders or across the House of Commons chamber. They were conflicts within my own group, waged in whispers down hallways, in late-night planning sessions, and in the shifting loyalties of men and women who had previously had a common goal but were now split apart by ambition and mistrust.

It takes both devotion and disagreement to be a party leader. I had risen from Lambeth's council chambers to the nation's highest office thanks to the Conservative Party. However, the party was already restless when I walked into Number Ten. For more than ten years, Margaret Thatcher had ruled it with an unwavering authority. My arrival was the uncomfortable compromise of a family forced to accept change after a long reign, rather than the joyous entry of a conquering hero. Many of my coworkers viewed me more as a caregiver filling the role of a higher authority than as a leader in my own right.

Before my time, the seeds of dissatisfaction had been sown. Fault lines had been forged by the concerns of Europe, the arguments over economic policy, and the fatigue of years of rule, and they were getting wider every year. Managing those fault lines and keeping a group together that frequently did not want to be kept together was my job. It was similar to trying to hold a bundle of twigs in hands that competitors were constantly prying open.

The most glaring rift between us was the Maastricht Treaty. For several Conservatives, it signified advancement and the strengthening of Britain's position in Europe. Others saw the ceding of sovereignty to anonymous bureaucrats as treachery. I was in the middle of the controversy, being accused of recklessness by one side and timidity by the other. I made an effort to remind them that compromise is not weakness but survival and that politics is rarely about absolutes. However, when conviction burns hot, well-reasoned statements frequently fall hollow.

Rebellion became a recurring theme. Every Commons vote became an exercise in my power. At times, I was aware that the faces on the other side of the aisle were more angry than the ones behind me as I stood at the dispatch box. Speaking to a chamber while even your allies are honing their skills is a lonely experience. We were characterized as a party at war with ourselves by the media, which is always looking for drama. I couldn't blame them. The proof was obvious.

Some of the attacks were personal, while others were political. Backbench rumors, deliberate press leaks, and queries presented by alleged allies rather than rivals all damaged not just my reputation but also my soul. A leader needs to master endurance. It takes a reservoir of patience that I occasionally questioned whether I had to get out of bed every morning and confront coworkers who plot at night and smile during the day. However, I discovered that reservoir in my recollections of adversity and in my belief that public service is more important than party politics.

Being a leader reveals a man's loneliness, which was one of the most agonizing things I ever learned. Although coworkers may applaud during a conference and publicly swear allegiance, this commitment frequently turns out to be conditional when circumstances change. I was aware that not all of my goals could be controlled. My only option was to uphold my morals and rule as fairly as the situation permitted. I made an effort to keep the government focused on issues that affected regular people, such as jobs, hospitals, and schools, even while the party split around me. I hoped that instead of focusing on the noise of our arguments, the public would evaluate us based on the actual accomplishments we made.

However, the sound got louder. Every uprising nourished the one after it. Every scandal no matter how small was exaggerated into a representation of deterioration. Like a permanent stain, the word "sleaze" started to cling to the gathering. Since I had always held the view that integrity is the cornerstone of public life, I was severely affected. However, I was also aware that perception may be just as harmful as reality. The suspicion persisted even after people were found not guilty. Furthermore, suspicion is frequently sufficient in politics.

I experimented with several tactics. I occasionally extended an olive branch to people who had betrayed me in an attempt to make amends. Other times, instead of sniping from the shadows, I opted for firmness and dared rebels to openly challenge me. Neither strategy resulted in enduring peace. The divisions were no longer merely tactical. They were emotional, ideological, and occasionally personal. With the world watching, the family that had formerly taken pride in its discipline was now embroiled in a heated quarrel over dinner.

I can't deny that I experienced depressing moments. It was depressing to witness the Disraeli-Churchill party degraded to trivial disputes. It hurts to be made fun of in the media and portrayed as weak. However, I was also aware that comfort is not a factor in leadership. It is about remaining steadfast in the face of ground tremors. I became more determined. I wouldn't light the match if they intended to ruin the celebration. Even if the crew rebelled, it was my responsibility to steer the ship through rough waves and save what could be saved.

In retrospect, I view those difficulties as the unavoidable tribulations of a long administration nearing the end of its natural existence, rather than as personal shortcomings. Parties tire out, differences deepen, and ambition intensifies. At the moment when all those forces came together, I was the leader. Whether I handled them successfully or poorly will be determined by history. All I know is that I gave it my all using the resources at my disposal and the belief that service must come before selfishness.

The Prolonged Journey to the 1997 Loss

A loss is never unexpected. Long before the last battle is fought, the march starts. The gradual deterioration of trust, the buildup of fatigue, and the ascent of an opponent who was adept at influencing public opinion marked the beginning of the march into 1997 rather than the fervor of an election campaign.

Our greatest pride, the aura of economic ability, was destroyed after Black Wednesday. The public's recollection was centered on the humiliation, even if the economy rebounded and prospered in many ways in the years that followed. They did not readily forgive since they felt deceived. No matter how good a policy was, it was always viewed through that distrustful prism. One of the worst facts of politics is that years of hard work can be overshadowed by a single event. The controversies also served their purpose. Respect was eroded by each headline. Whether real or fabricated, every tale of improper behavior served to support a narrative of deterioration. I made an effort to respond by presenting the facts, proposing changes, and arguing for justice. However, it is difficult to change a tale once the public has decided on it. We were no longer regarded as the prosperous and disciplined party. We were perceived as worn out, split, and weakened.

In the meantime, Labour had selected a new leader who was the complete reverse of who we were. Tony Blair's message was disciplined, youthful, and full of energy. He talked about modernization, rebirth, and a Britain prepared to enter a new era. His image and his words were carefully controlled. The people, fed up with our arguments, recognized potential in him. The fact that a large portion of his program was still unclear did not matter. The important thing was that we looked stale, and he looked fresh.

I put a lot of attention into the years before 1997. I spoke to towns around the nation and made an effort to demonstrate that the government was still paying attention. Despite the press's preference to concentrate on party infighting, I took pride in my efforts on peace in Northern Ireland. I advocated for public service changes. All of these attempts, however, felt like filling a barrel with holes with water. The more I drank, the more cynicism drained away.

The divides within the party deepened. The vast wedge was still Europe. A few of my coworkers urged me to adopt a more assertive stance, promising referendums and declaring independence from Brussels. Others urged me to advance integration in order to guarantee Britain's position at the heart of Europe. Since I thought it was the only responsible course of action, I made an effort to maintain the middle ground. The middle ground, however, may occasionally feel like quicksand in politics. You sink more when you stand more securely.

I was aware that the chances were against us as the election drew near. According to opinion polls, Labour had a significant lead. Inevitability, the media said. But before the competition started, I wouldn't give up. Campaigns are unpredictable. The general public can be erratic. I thought there could still be a possibility if we offered a program of consistency and experience.

The 1997 campaign was a fierce battle. I spoke in factories, schools, and hallways while traveling nonstop. I reminded people of our accomplishments, the economy's recovery, Britain's continued international respect, and the possibility of peace in Northern Ireland. However, the tone was established. I felt it at every stop. The audiences were cool and kind. The certainty of continuity was outweighed by the desire for change.

The decision was delivered with brutal clarity on election night. Red seats turned out to be secure for decades. Colleagues who sacrificed their life for the party lost what they had spent decades building in a matter of hours. It was the largest defeat in our history. As I sat in my constituency, I listened to the results roll in, each one dealing a blow to the party's organization. I was both saddened and relieved when the final count verified our fears.

I was saddened because I realized how much hard work had been undone by the lack of unity and image. The long march of struggle was over, which was a relief. Clarity comes from defeat. It finishes the tiresome chapters and puts a stop to the never-ending struggles. It permits relaxation, introspection, and rejuvenation. For me, it signaled that my tenure as prime minister was coming to a close. It required the party to face its differences. It signified a new era for the nation under new leadership.

It was with no resentment when I walked out of Downing Street for the last time. I'd contribute what I could. My workplace had weathered storms that could have destroyed weaker vessels. Yes, I had erred, but I had also upheld the values of integrity and service. The populace had made a different decision. That is a democratic right. A leader's responsibility is to accept, not to hold on, to turn over the keys with honor, and to wish the nation well.

In retrospect, I view the march toward 1997 as a lesson as well as a failure. Power does not last forever. In a day, one's reputation can be destroyed. Voters will admonish parties who lose their sense of humility. However, if one has served honorably, there is honor even in defeat.

I knew going out of government that history would occasionally criticize my time. However, I was also aware that my story was not about a man who pursued greatness for its own sake, but rather about a man who rose from lowly origins and carried the burden of the greatest position with all the integrity he could summon. That's still sufficient in my opinion.

Chapter 6: Life After Downing Street and Legacy

New Horizons and Premiership Retirement

For the first time in seven years, John Major was no longer the prime leader of Britain when the door of Number Ten closed behind him in the spring of 1997. A mixture of relief and sadness weighed heavily on that moment. He had endured the relentless demands of the government for years, where each hour belonged to the state rather than to himself. The weight vanished abruptly, leaving behind an emptiness that only those who have left the greatest stage can understand.

Major's retirement from Downing Street was not like some of his predecessors' booming exits. His hand was not forced by controversy or a precipitous slide. Instead, it marked the silent conclusion of a protracted period in which popular sentiment had decisively shifted in favor of Labour and Tony Blair. He was characterized by the media as gracious in defeat, and on that last day, he did indeed conduct himself with dignity. Even if the nation disapproved of his party, it did not completely turn against him. He was viewed by many as a guy who had honestly, if not always stylishly, carried unachievable burdens.

There were fresh possibilities in life after Downing Street. John Major was finally able to wake up without the red boxes that were stacked up next to his bed for the first time in decades. He didn't have to worry about what may happen in the Commons by noon when he read the morning papers. He could return to cricket matches, go for long walks, and experience the normalcy of life. However, Major was not a man who was meant to be idle. Despite laying down the crown, he refused to withdraw into silence since service had molded him.

For a few more years, he continued to serve as the Huntingdon representative in parliament, standing in for the people who had originally trusted him long before the country knew him. Although he was no longer the person in charge of government business at the dispatch box and spoke less regularly in the Commons, his remarks were nonetheless weighed heavily by his expertise. He contributed to discussions where honesty was more important than popularity.

He started looking into roles outside of the Commons. Writing, business, and diplomacy all have their own allure. When his memoirs were released in 1999, they showed the unvarnished thoughts of a man who had seen both victories and setbacks. It contained a note of moderation, an attempt to correct the record without settling scores, in contrast to many political memoirs that are dripping with resentment. The same quiet tenacity that had characterized his years in power was evident to readers in those pages.

The world at large opened its doors as well. He was asked to give lectures at universities. His advice on diplomacy and governance was sought by international organizations. His patronage was welcomed by charities. Major found a freedom in leaving office that he had never experienced before, an opportunity to mold his post-premiership into a new season of service rather than a retreat.

An Introspective and Honest Voice in Public Life

In the years following Downing Street, Major stood out for the way his voice maintained its authority in the absence of the apparatus of power. Many previous leaders become parodies of themselves or fade into obscurity. Rather, Major developed into an elder statesman. He gave fewer speeches, but when he did, the country paid attention.

He frequently spoke on the topic of political integrity. He spoke about the necessity of decency in public life with unusual clarity, having weathered the storms of sleaze accusations in his own government. He reminded the country that respect is the cornerstone of democracy and not a sign of weakness when the political discourse becomes nasty. He exhorted colleagues from all walks of life to prioritize country above party and service over dogma.

His remarks were especially relevant in the discussions about Britain's position in Europe. Even though he was no longer in charge of making decisions, he consistently spoke about the risks of isolation. He felt that Britain was more powerful when involved, when influencing Europe's course rather than ignoring it. Though they weren't always well received, his cautions about the dangers of division were given with conviction and without malice. Even his detractors acknowledged that he spoke from principle rather than ambition.

At a period when skepticism was becoming more prevalent, Major also spoke up for democratic institutions. He reminded audiences that even when governments make mistakes, the accountability and representation system is still a valuable asset that should be protected. He promoted the traits that had distinguished his own leadership and those he felt were crucial for Britain's future: moderation, listening, and compromise.

The fact that he had nothing to gain might have been the driving force behind his musings. He could talk plainly and was no longer running for office. His voice frequently rose above the din, steady and calm, when political divisions or scandals shook the country. John Major became a unique individual in a world full of sharp elbows and soundbites, an unbiased observer of the limitations and possibilities of public life.

Charitable Contributions and Humanitarian Activities

Major focused his energies on causes that were near and dear to his heart after being released from the daily grind of government. He had a lifelong empathy for the poor because of his upbringing. He had experienced the coldness of want and the burden of limited opportunities as a child growing up in poverty. His philanthropic endeavors were influenced by that memory.

He got involved with a variety of humanitarian organizations, contributing his name and time to projects aimed at helping the underprivileged. One of his main concerns was education. He supported initiatives that gave kids from underprivileged homes more access to education. He maintained that a child's future shouldn't be dictated by their parents' financial situation. He saw education as more than just a policy; it was his lifeline and the reason he had ascended from the council estate to the Westminster corridors.

His patronage also helped health charities. He was a tireless champion for organizations that support carers, cancer research, and cardiac care. He met with families whose lives were impacted by disease, raised money, and attended events. He approached as a man who cared, listened, and asked questions rather than as a remote dignitary.

He backed initiatives for conflict resolution and development on a global scale. He had learned about the human cost of war from his experiences in Northern Ireland and the Gulf War. Since he thought that peace is created not only via treaties but also through shared wealth, schools, and clinics, he promoted funding for aid and diplomacy. Although his efforts frequently went unreported in the media, it subtly altered lives.

His lifetime love of cricket offered another opportunity to contribute. He was elected president of the MCC after serving as president of the Surrey County Cricket Club. Even so, he made use of the position for purposes other than athletics. He praised cricket's ability to promote harmony and understanding because he saw it as a game that united Commonwealth nations and served as a bridge between cultures.

The same sense of duty that had driven him into politics was evident in all of these endeavors. Withdrawal was not synonymous with retirement. It required moving the service from Westminster's opulent theatre to neighborhood charity halls and get-togethers.

John Major's Lasting Influence on British History

It is rare for legacies to be written in the present. They are formed over time by the gradual reevaluation of successes and setbacks after the day's passions have subsided. The years after his premiership have given John Major the opportunity to see things more clearly.

He was frequently overlooked while in office. He didn't have his predecessor's charm or his successor's youthful glitz. He was perceived as banal, gray, and even uninteresting. His strength, however, resided in that banality. As a leader, he was aware of the hardships faced by common Britons, having experienced them himself. He ruled patiently rather than with thunder. His goal was to serve, not to shine.

His contribution to the peace process in Northern Ireland stands as one of his most enduring accomplishments. Major set important foundations that others would later build upon in the Good Friday Agreement. The groundwork for peace was established by his tenacity in covert negotiations, his readiness to assume political risks, and his conviction that communication must go on despite conflict. His calm bravery over those years is now recognized by history.

He lived through a period of economic upheaval and recovery. Although Black Wednesday had a lasting impact, his administration was responsible for bringing growth back and controlling inflation. The economy was stronger than the general public believed when Labour came to power in 1997. In retrospect, Major is credited by some economists with creating the framework for the stability of the decade that followed.

In terms of culture, he advocated for compassion and inclusivity. He frequently talked about a Britain that was comfortable with itself, one that valued justice and variety. His administration launched the National Lottery, which has subsequently provided funding for innumerable communal and cultural initiatives. He supported local projects and citizens' rights because he thought that strong communities are the foundation of a successful nation.

His example of integrity is another aspect of his legacy. Even if his government was marred by other people's misdeeds, Major remained personally untarnished. His reputation for honesty remained intact after he left government. That in itself sets him apart in a political moment where cynicism is common.

Most significantly, his life narrative serves as motivation. The youngster who sold garden gnomes at his father's stall, grew up in poverty, and left school with minimal credentials went on to become the leader of Britain. His path serves as evidence that fate need not be predetermined by birth in a democracy. His tale gives encouragement to innumerable young people who are struggling by showing that morality and hard work may still lead to the top positions in the country.

Ultimately, bombastic speech and theatrical gestures fail to adequately convey John Major's legacy. It can be found in perseverance, the silent dignity of service, and the conviction that, despite its mess and cruelty, politics can be a great vocation. He may not have been a brilliant light, but he maintained the integrity of the flame in a time when it was dwindling dangerously.

History will therefore remember him. Not as the most brilliant star among British presidents, but as someone who steadily led his country in the face of adversity. a man who came into office in the dark, who walked through storms that would have destroyed others, and who came out of them untarnished. John Major lives on in Britain's history as a lesson that greatness can appear modest.

Printed in Dunstable, United Kingdom